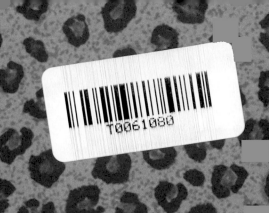

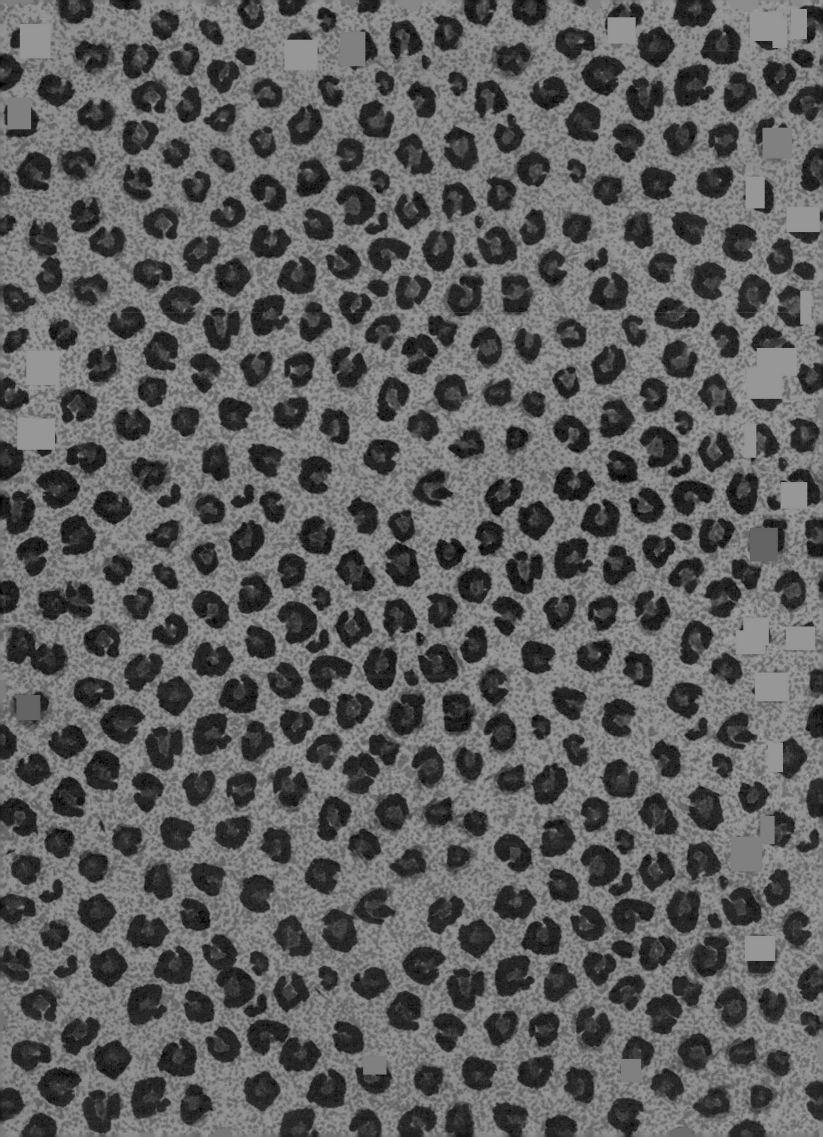

A BOOK of CATS

At home with cats around the world

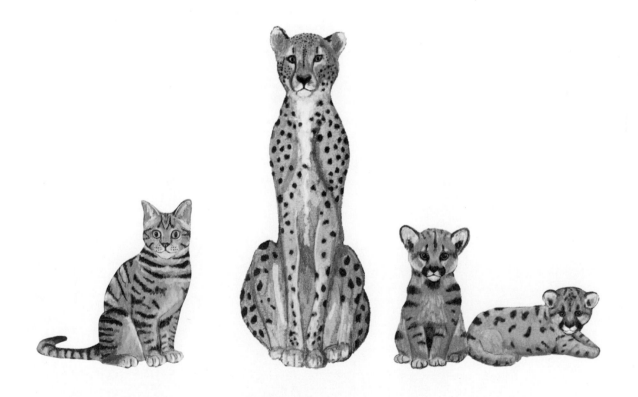

Katie Viggers

Laurence King Publishing

For team Huggers

LAURENCE KING

First published in Great Britain in 2021 by Laurence King Publishing

1 3 5 7 9 10 8 6 4 2

Text and illustrations © Katie Viggers 2021
Additional text by Isabel Thomas
Designed by Renata Latipova

A CIP catalog record for this book is available from the British Library.

ISBN 978-1-91394-724-8

Printed and bound in China

Laurence King Publishing
An imprint of
Hachette Children's Group
Part of Hodder and Stoughton
Carmelite House
50 Victoria Embankment
London EC4Y 0DZ

An Hachette UK Company
www.hachette.co.uk
www.hachettechildrens.co.uk

www.laurenceking.com

Laurence King Publishing is committed to ethical and sustainable production. We are proud participants in The Book Chain Project®

BOOK CHAIN PROJECT

Contents

Meet the cats

There are almost 40 different species of cats. All of them have bendy, agile bodies, long tails, and sharp teeth and claws.

Cats come in all different sizes: big cats, smaller cats, and house cats. Let's meet the cat family!

Us cats don't all live in the same place, we just got together to help make this book.

Snow leopard

Lion

Jaguar

Pet cat

Leopard

Cougar

Cheetah

Tiger

Cheetahs
Acinonyx jubatus

Africa is home to around 7,100 wild cheetahs. They like to live in grassy plains and deserts.

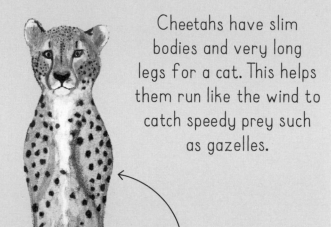

Cheetahs have slim bodies and very long legs for a cat. This helps them run like the wind to catch speedy prey such as gazelles.

Their most famous feature is their spotty coat.

KING CHEETAH
King cheetahs have softer fur, with stripes as well as spots. Only around ten are thought to live in the wild, making them some of the world's rarest animals.

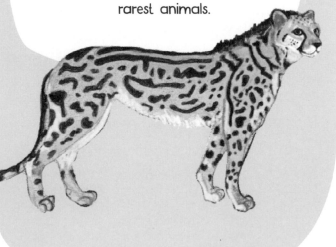

When it comes to exercise, you can't beat a cheetah. Join us at the cheetah gym!

Amazing eyesight helps cheetahs spot prey moving in long grass.

The black "tear marks" running down a cheetah's face are called malar stripes. They soak up sunlight, so the cheetah doesn't get dazzled.

Many cats hunt at dawn or dusk, but cheetahs are most active in the day. Prey can see them coming in the bright sunlight, so cheetahs can't creep up and pounce. Instead, they rely on overtaking prey in a high-speed chase.

It's a record!

Cheetahs sprint at up to 70 miles per hour, making them the fastest animals on land.

Cheetahs aren't able to keep up this incredible speed for very long, which is why they end up empty-pawed after most chases.

Lions *Panthera leo*

Lions have a fearsome reputation, but they can be big softies—and not just because of their fluffy manes!

Male lions are the only cats with bushy manes. They start to grow when a lion is three years old and can be lots of different colors, from black to golden.

AFRICAN LION
Around 20,000 African lions live in the wild. African lions are the most sociable big cats. They live in large family groups called prides.

A lion's mane makes it look bigger. This helps to scare away other lions who might want to take over their pride.

KEEP OUT
(OR ELSE)

ASIATIC LION
Asiatic lions are smaller and rarer. There are only around 500 left in the wild. They live in a single forested area in northwest India.

Their manes are smaller and often darker.

LIONESS
Female lions hunt in groups. With teamwork, they can tackle very large animals like cape buffaloes, zebras, and even giraffes. Mother lions look after their cubs until they are at least 16 months old. They help feed other cubs too.

Tigers
Panthera tigris

Tigers are the biggest of the big cats and they are also the most dangerous!

Tigers live in different areas of Asia, from tropical forests to snowy mountains. They are hard to spot, because fewer than 4,000 tigers still live in the wild.

The largest tigers measure more than ten feet from nose to tail. That's as long as a small car!

SIBERIAN TIGER
Siberian tigers live in cold places. They have thick fur to keep them warm, and large paws to pad across the snow.

SUMATRAN TIGER
One island in Indonesia is home to all the Sumatran tigers in the world. They are the smallest tigers of all.

BENGAL TIGER
Bengal tigers are the most common tigers. Not all have bright orange fur. Sometimes a Bengal tiger is born with white fur.

SABER-TOOTHED TIGER
Don't worry, you'll never bump into a saber-toothed tiger. These prehistoric cats became extinct around 10,000 years ago. They weren't really tigers, but more closely related to clouded leopards.

Each of their canine teeth was longer than a pencil!

When we're not eating animals like antelope or buffalo, we like canned Tiger Food as a treat!

No two tigers share the same pattern of stripes. Like our fingerprints, they are unique.

Tigers are excellent climbers, jumpers, and swimmers. Young tigers like to play and cool down in the water too.

Cougars
Puma concolor

Let's head to the Americas to meet some large cats that are not technically big cats!

Cougars mainly live in the mountains of North and South America. They're happy to live in forests, grasslands, and swamps too—as long as there are plenty of places to hide.

Humans and other cougars are the main animals they hide from, though young or sick cougars also need to watch out for wolves and bears!

Short, sturdy legs and a bushy tail help cougars balance as they climb into the best hiding places.

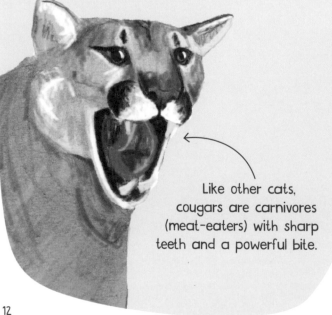

Like other cats, cougars are carnivores (meat-eaters) with sharp teeth and a powerful bite.

Cougars have a lot of different names. They are sometimes called mountain lions, pumas, panthers, or catamounts. But what names would they choose for themselves?

I'm called Lady Lily.

CUBS

Baby cats are known as cubs or kittens, and cougar cubs are some of the cutest. They stick with their mother for up to two years, learning to hunt and hide.

Leopards
Panthera pardus

Leopards live in more parts of the world than any other type of cat.

A leopard's spots are really rosettes of black fur. Sometimes the shape of their spots can tell you where they're from.

AFRICAN LEOPARD
Leopards in East Africa have circular spots. In South Africa, the spots are shaped more like squares!

Most leopards live in the woodlands and grasslands of Africa. They have to compete with lions for the same food.

AMUR LEOPARD
The Amur leopard is the world's rarest. Fewer than 80 still live in the wild. Thick fur keeps them warm in their cold Russian forest home.

SNOW LEOPARD
Snow leopards survive in the frozen mountains of Central Asia.

Snow leopards are perfectly suited to life on steep mountain slopes, with thick fur and a bushy tail to keep them warm.

To stay safe from lions, leopards try to hunt at different times of day. Trees are also a safe hiding (and sleeping) place.

Snow leopards love to sneak up on other animals, such as mountain ibex. Watch out for the horns!

Jaguars *Panthera onca*

Jaguars love to hunt and hide among the trees.

Jaguars are found in Central and South America, Mexico, and some parts of the southern United States too. The best place to spot them is near the Amazon River in South America. Sunrise and sunset are their favorite times to hunt.

Jaguars have the strongest bite of any cat.

BLACK PANTHERS
Some jaguars have completely black coats and are known as black panthers. They even have black spots, but it's hard to see them. Confusingly, leopards with black coats are also known as black panthers.

Despite their name, jaguars are almost never seen driving classic cars.

We are the Jaguar Cadets. When we're not resting, we're practicing our hunting skills on the jungle assault course.

Jaguars are good at climbing, swimming, and crawling. They are stealthy enough to creep up on almost any prey—from deer and snakes, to turtles and fish.

"SPOT" THE DIFFERENCE

Jaguars have rosettes with small spots inside.

Leopards have rosettes with darker fur inside.

Cheetahs have solid round spots.

Jaguars love water. In fact, they are rarely found living in a place without a river, stream, lagoon, or swamp.

Wild cats

Smaller cats have lots in common with big cats. They have similar features and they move and hunt in the same way too. But there is one "cat" on this page that doesn't belong here. Can you spot the impostor?

PALLAS'S CAT
Otocolobus manul

These Central Asian cats are small but look larger thanks to their thick, woolly fur. They have extra eyelids that can be closed when their habitat gets too cold or dusty.

IBERIAN LYNX
Lynx pardinus

These small lynxes are unmistakable with their ear tufts and large face ruffs. They are also very rare, living in just two small areas of Spain.

BORNEO BAY CAT
Catopuma badia

This mysterious cat is about the size of a house cat, but with dark brown-red fur and black markings. Only a few have ever been spotted.

CARACAL
Caracal caracal

Found in Africa, the Middle East, and South Asia, these characterful cats are known for their awesome ear tufts. Their ears can twitch to help them communicate.

MEERKAT

Despite their name, meerkats are a type of mongoose, with no relation to the cat family.

BOBCAT
Lynx rufus

Bobcats are very common in North America. Their name comes from their short, "bobbed" tails.

WORLD'S SMALLEST CATS

BLACK-FOOTED CAT
Felis nigripes

Africa's smallest cat is also one of the smallest in the world. The bottoms of their feet are hairy, to protect them as they walk across hot sand.

RUSTY-SPOTTED CAT
Prionailurus rubiginosus

The smallest of the wild cats lives in India and Sri Lanka. They have reddish streaks and spots on their faces and coats.

SERVAL
Leptailurus serval

With large ears and long legs, these African wild cats can bound up to six feet high. They use sound to locate small animals in the long grass–and then they pounce!

I said pounce, not bounce.

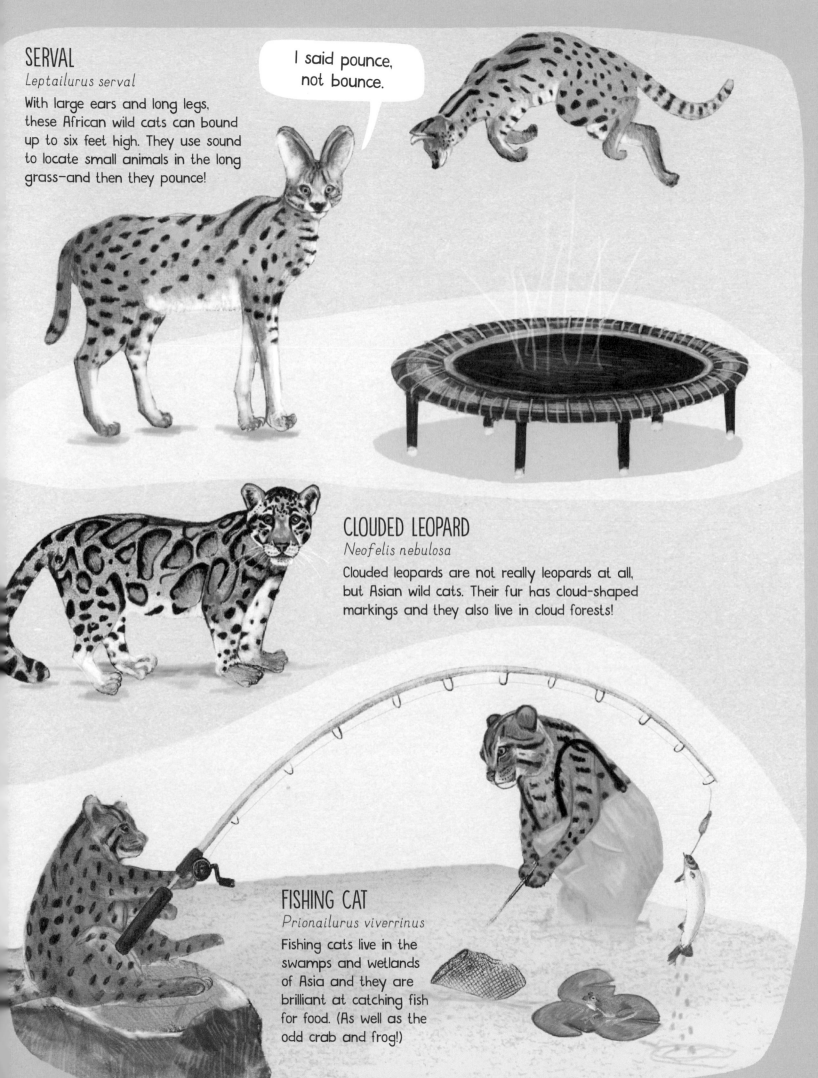

CLOUDED LEOPARD
Neofelis nebulosa

Clouded leopards are not really leopards at all, but Asian wild cats. Their fur has cloud-shaped markings and they also live in cloud forests!

FISHING CAT
Prionailurus viverrinus

Fishing cats live in the swamps and wetlands of Asia and they are brilliant at catching fish for food. (As well as the odd crab and frog!)

House cats

Humans have been keeping pet cats for 4,000 years. The first cat lovers were the ancient Egyptians. Cats helped to catch mice and rats around their homes.

MAINE COON

There are more than 70 breeds of house cat. The Maine Coon is the largest.

SIAMESE

Siamese cats love attention and curling up in warm places.

EXOTIC SHORTHAIR

You can't miss this cat's flat nose and large eyes.

SPHYNX

Sphynx cats have soft skin with barely any fur.

BENGAL

The Bengal cat's ancestors include Asian leopard cats. Its coat has leopard-like rosettes.

SCOTTISH FOLD

These cats have kittens with straight ears. After three weeks, the ears fold down.

RAGDOLL

The ragdoll has a reputation for being chilled out.

MOGGY

Cats that are a mixture of different breeds are known as moggies. They are the most common pet cats.

House cats often behave like their wild relatives...

They like to chase and catch animals—although their prey is usually a little smaller.

They like to climb trees—and only get stuck *sometimes.*

They like nothing better than a cat-nap in a cozy place.

They can be fierce (when they need to).

Just like big cats, house cats love to stretch and flex their claws.

But they are NOT fond of getting wet. You won't see a house cat go for a swim.

I'm working on my yoga poses.

Eating

Cats are carnivores (meat-eaters). They don't need to eat any fruit or vegetables at all. The bigger the cat, the bigger the prey it can catch.

Cats begin by stalking their prey. They hide and watch, sometimes creeping closer. Some wild cats pounce on prey in a single leap. Others chase the prey and tackle it to the ground. Then it's time for a big feast!

House cats have food served to them by their owners. Most eat canned cat food, but some get lovely home-cooked meals.

Jaguars can catch food that lives in water, such as snakes and small crocodilians.

Yikes!

Tigers are not picky eaters. They will try anything, from ants to water buffalo.

Camouflage

Blending in with the background helps cats to hunt. Each cat has a coat that provides the right kind of camouflage for where it lives.

Spots or "rosettes" break up the outline of both jaguars and leopards.

I like to hide in boxes.

A tiger's orange and black stripes provide surprisingly good camouflage in tall grasses.

Roaring

A roar is a deep cry or call that travels long distances, and it is frightening no matter how far away you are! Only big cats can roar, but all cats make sounds of some kind.

A lion's roar is about 25 times louder than a lawnmower. It's the loudest of any big cat and can be heard 5 miles away!

ROAR

Most small wild cats (and house cats) can purr. They can also meow.

meow

PURRR

ROAR

Although cheetahs are big, they are built more like small cats and can't roar. But they can purr!

Jaguars can roar (but not as loudly as lions).

A tiger's roar is so scary it can stop prey in their tracks. This probably makes them easier to catch!

ROAR

Snow leopards make an unusual sound that's a cross between a meow and a roar. This yowling noise lets other snow leopards know where they are.

YOWL

A leopard's roar sounds just like a saw being used to cut wood!

ROAR

Hisss

Cougars make loud screeching or screaming noises. They can also purr and hiss.

Cats use softer sounds around their cubs or kittens, such as snorts, chirps, and chirrups.

Sleeping

The cat family includes some of the sleepiest predators in the world. Most cats are crepuscular, which means they do most of their moving, hunting, and eating at dawn and dusk. It also means they can be caught catching up on sleep at any time of day or night.

Snow leopards have a built-in duvet—their fluffy tails.

Cheetahs can be spotted hunting in the daytime, while their competition is sitting in the shade.

They use up so much energy in a chase, they often need a power nap afterward!

Just seeing if you're awake!

House cats are often spotted dozing in the day. Unlike other cats, they have a habit of being most active at night.

Hunting at dawn means an early start for lions, but they can then relax during the hottest part of the day.

Leopards often hunt at night, when they can creep up on sleeping baboons! To make sure the same doesn't happen to them, they snooze by day in the safety of a tree.

Tigers and jaguars are more likely to sleep whenever and wherever they want. That could be at any time, on a branch, a rock, or curled up on the ground.

Lions and tigers are the laziest big cats, sleeping for up to 20 hours a day.

Cat map

These are the places you're most likely to find the cats in this book. Some cats live in different habitats in lots of different countries, while others are found in just one forest or national park.

NORTH AMERICA
Small and medium-sized wild cats are widespread in North America. The bobcat is one of the most common. It is found in all kinds of different habitats.

EUROPE
Europe was once home to many different types of wild cats, but today they are rare. The Iberian lynx has such a small amount of natural habitat left that it is endangered.

SOUTH AMERICA
South America is home to just one big cat—the jaguar, including black panthers. Its smaller wild cats include cougars, ocelots, and Andean cats.

AFRICA
Africa is home to many types of cats, big and small. Lions are the most famous, and the only cats to live in groups.

HOUSE CATS
Cats are kept as pets on every continent. Some domestic cats also live in the wild and survive by hunting or scavenging. They are known as feral cats.

ASIA

Asia is home to a huge range of different cats, including tigers and even a small population of lions. Some are specially adapted to live in just one habitat. Others, such as leopards, have a wider range.

AUSTRALASIA

Other than pets, the only cats in Australasia are feral house cats. They cause problems for local wildlife, which has adapted over millions of years without cats around. These local birds, reptiles, fish, mammals, and insects are not good at defending themselves from a cat's hunting skills.

ANTARCTICA

Cats don't naturally live in Antarctica. The continent is so cold, it has no land mammals at all! However, humans have taken many house cats to Antarctica. They were carried on board explorers' ships and fishing boats to catch rats that would eat the crew's food.

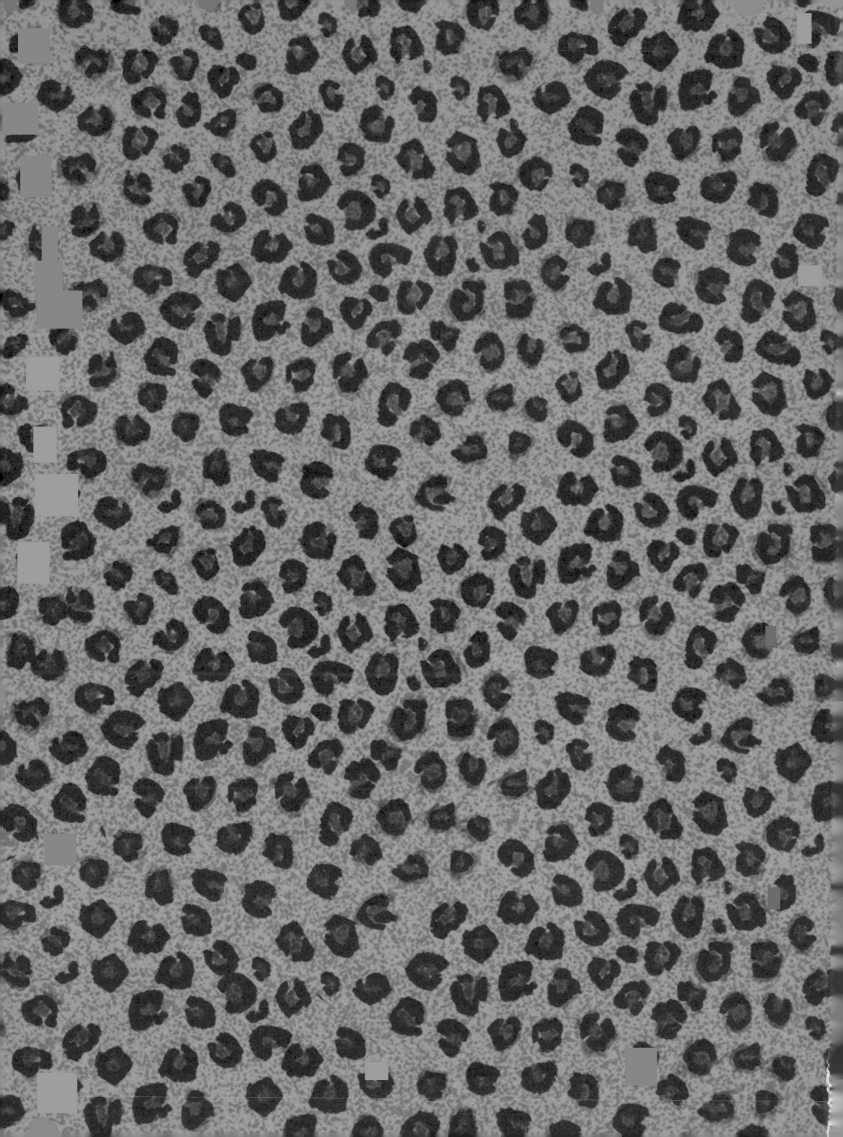